Y0-ARR-297

FONTANA
POCKET LIBRARY OF GREAT ART

Plate 1. SELF-PORTRAIT. *About 1886. Pencil*
The Art Institute of Chicago (Arthur Heun Fund)

PAUL

CEZANNE

(1839–1906)

text by

THEODORE ROUSSEAU, JR.
Curator of Paintings
The Metropolitan Museum of Art, New York

COLLINS
Fontana Pocket Library of Great Art

On the cover
TULIPS AND APPLES *(see color plate 22)*

Published in co-operation with Harry Abrams, N.V., Amsterdam, Holland, 1954

Plate 2. STUDY OF ORANGES. *1895-1900. Water color*
Collection Carroll S. Tyson, Philadelphia

P. Cezanne

Cézanne devoted his life entirely to painting. It was not until his last years that he was understood and admired by a small group of painters and one or two far-sighted collectors and dealers. But in the half-century which has passed since his death, his influence has dominated almost every movement of modern painting.

He was born in 1839 in Aix-en-Provence, a provincial town in southern France. His father, a self-made man, started as a hat maker and became one of the most prominent bankers of the town. It was thanks to the money he left his family that Paul was able to continue painting in spite of his failure to sell any of his work until just before the end of his life. His father had wanted him to enter the family business and sent him to law school. But the boy had made up his mind to be a painter; and after many family arguments, and one false start, he was given an allowance and sent to study art in Paris.

There he joined Emile Zola, his closest boyhood friend, and together they became part of the group of young artists who lived the Bohemian life and planned to revolutionize the traditions of painting. Among their friends were the men who have become famous as the greatest painters of their day: Manet, Degas, Renoir, and Monet.

Cézanne worked in Paris or in the country nearby and spent much time with his friends in the cafés theorizing about the "new" style of painting. Each year he submitted a painting to the Salon, but he was always turned down. He also showed his work in the independent exhibitions which his group of friends organized and which earned for them the name "Impressionists." Not only the critics, but also the public laughed at the paintings; and with the exception of an isolated few, no one understood them. People of every period in history have certain visual habits acquired from what they are used to seeing around them; and in the second half of the nineteenth century, these habits were formed by the works of the old masters, discolored and darkened by yellow varnish, and by the Salon painters who imitated them. As a result, the bright colors used by the young painters seemed harsh, and their fresh, unconventional drawing awkward. Cézanne's paintings, perhaps because of their intense conviction, attracted more attention, and drew more abuse and ridicule than those of the other members of the group. The hostility of both critics and public was among the most important factors in Cézanne's life and had a profound effect on his character and painting. He returned to Aix and, except for occasional trips to Paris, he remained there until his death in 1906.

He took his profession very seriously, as seriously as

Plate 3. Below: ECORCHE (FLAYED MAN), *an anatomical study figure once attributed to Michelangelo At left:* A STUDY BY CEZANNE AFTER THE ECORCHE. *About 1890 Pencil. The Art Institute of Chicago (Arthur Heun Fund)*

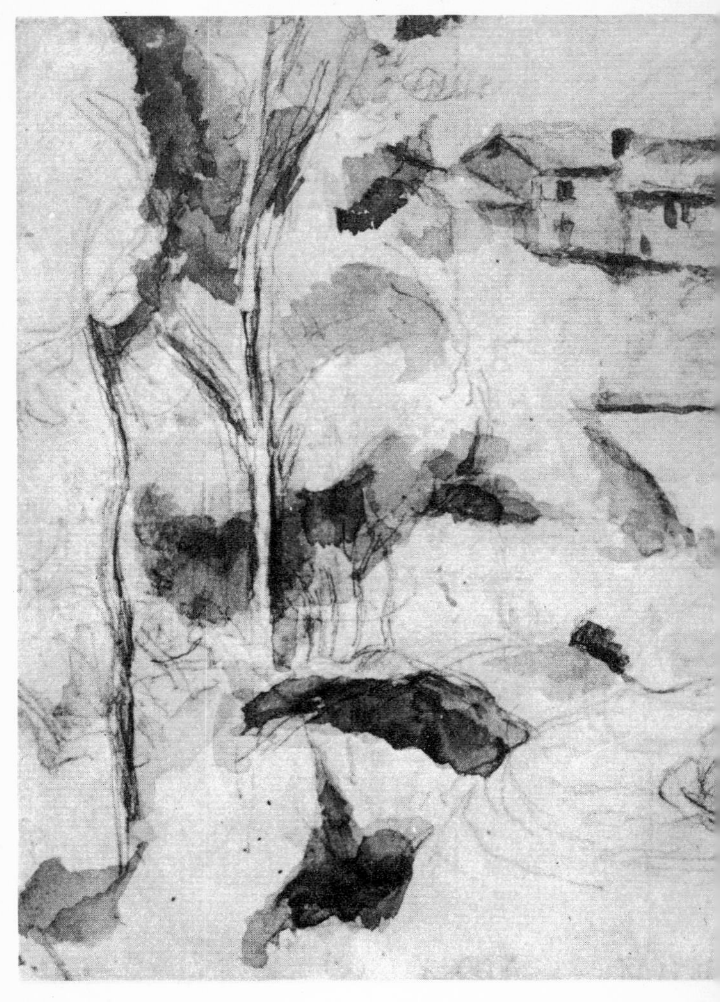

Plate 4. THE BRIDGE AT GARDANNE. *1885-86. Water color. Museum*

lern Art, New York (Lillie P. Bliss Collection)

any businessman, doctor, or lawyer, devoting himself exclusively to it and working with tremendous energy. His integrity was absolute, and he made no concessions to public taste or fashion at any time in his life. Deeply cultivated and widely read, he related all his artistic experiences, whether musical or literary, to painting. Far from wishing to break with tradition, he respected it and ceaselessly studied the work of the old masters, copying and sketching in the Louvre daily when he was in Paris. His chief ambition was to add his own contribution to the great tradition of painting. The complete failure of all but a few artists and friends to understand even the seriousness of his purpose was a terrible shock to him. He withdrew increasingly into himself until he became a misanthrope and almost a hermit.

Fortunately, he never completely lost his belief in himself, and his paintings bear witness to his profound conviction as to the importance of what he was doing. His early work is full of exuberance and romanticism, with a tendency to overstatement. Then for a while he worked under the influence of Impressionism, but he soon became aware of its structural weaknesses and began to subject himself to severe self-discipline. His mature paintings, for which he has become famous, are carefully planned and methodically constructed. If they are compared with the work of other painters, Cézanne's pictures strike us by their simplicity and directness. They do not invite us to enter into them and move from one element to another as do the Dutch little masters, for instance. They put over their message in a single statement like a fresco by Giotto.

His choice of subject matter was surprisingly limited. Within the usual categories of portraits, landscape, still life, and figure composition, he chose certain arrangements and concentrated on them, repeating them over and over again with slight variations. The subject was important to him chiefly as a means of expressing a

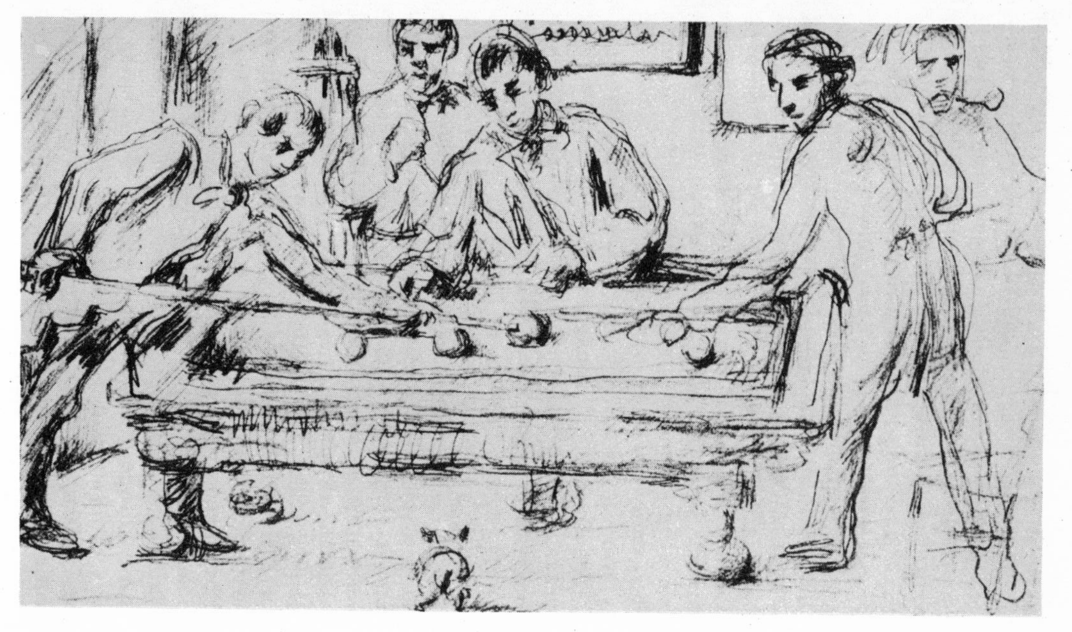

Plate 5. GAME OF BILLIARDS. *1870-75. Pencil. Collection the artist's family, Paris*

mood. A landscape may be serene or gay or have a real sense of tragedy; even a still life made up of everyday objects will give out a feeling of grandeur and austerity. His portraits, though at first sight aloof and distant, are remarkably sensitive to the emotional state of the sitter.

The final and permanent quality of Cézanne's compositions is due in great part to their concentrated unity. Regardless of any traditionally accepted rules, such as those of scientific perspective, the different parts of the painting are rearranged so that they complement each other and build up to a compact architectural structure standing solidly on its own. This is true whether the picture is considered as a flat surface or as a scene in depth. Even his many uncompleted paintings show these traits. In their clarity and order, combined with inner vitality, his compositions belong to the great classical tradition.

Fundamentally, Cézanne's nature was passionate and romantic, and it was through color that he expressed his true feelings. Among the old masters, he always proclaimed his preference for the great colorists: Titian, Tintoretto, Veronese, Rubens, Delacroix. His statements on color could be taken as a key to his method: "Everything is in the composition of the colors. Go to the Louvre and see. That is how Veronese composes." He was most sensitive to the expressive power of color and used it as the dominant factor in establishing the mood of his pictures. He spoke of the "colors of friendship," of "evil color," and of how by "marrying a shade of green to a red, one can either sadden a cheek or make it smile." The luminosity and infinite variety of his color is remarkable. Most other painters mix a local tone and apply it throughout a given passage. Cézanne seems to create a subtle change in almost every brush stroke. Thanks to this, each square inch of his canvas has vitality. There is never a flat, dull passage. In this, he is akin to the great colorists he admired, but his particular method is his own

Plate 6. Above: Detail from Rubens' LANDING OF MARIE DE MEDICIS, *with (below) Cézanne's study therefrom. About 1882. Pencil Collection the artist's family, Paris*

and remains one of the most original aspects of his art.

Line, pure abstract line, unlike anything in nature, is an important part of Cézanne's method. It gives accent to shapes, such as folds of drapery, tree trunks, or mountains. Sometimes he draws several lines with the brush, usually with blue pigment, all repeating the outline and resulting in a curious effect of visual vibration which gives added life to a particular color passage.

Like El Greco, Cézanne used his brush stroke both as a means of emphasizing the structure of his picture and of giving vitality to its surface. Sometimes movement is given to the composition by the general direction of the strokes. Sometimes differences of texture are brought out, not by an imitation of reality but by a change of stroke in contrast to adjacent areas. Different moods are also brought out, free and gay, quiet and orderly, harsh and violent. To the lover of Cézanne's paintings, this is one of their most enjoyable qualities.

Each of these elements was studied for its effect with infinite care. No painter was more methodical than Cézanne. In this respect, he comes close to Dürer and stands at the opposite pole from the carefree facility of Velasquez or the passionate outbursts of Van Gogh. He spent many more hours looking and thinking than he did painting. People who watched him say that he sometimes waited as long as twenty minutes between two strokes of his brush. He himself said that there were days when he looked at his subject so long that he felt "as if his eyes were bleeding." Some pictures took months to finish.

Despite their simplicity there is nothing obvious or poster-like about them. They must be looked at again and again with sustained attention before they completely reveal their beauty. But like other things in life which require real effort, they are the more richly rewarding because of it and offer an endless source of enjoyment to those who are willing to take the trouble.

Plate 7. NUDE WOMAN. *About 1895. Wash drawing*
The Louvre, Paris

Plate 8. THE RAPE. *1875-76. Pencil. The Art Institute of Chicago (Arthur Heun Fund)*

COLOR PLATES

PLATE 9

Painted about 1866

UNCLE DOMINIC AS A MONK

Collection Mr. and Mrs. Ira Haupt, New York

25⅝ x 21¼"

This portrait is a typical example of Cézanne's youthful work. His uncle posed for him dressed up as a monk in a white cowl, and one feels that the young artist enjoyed painting the picture in which there is a certain sardonic humor underlying the theatrical effect. The idea of this forceful and sensual-looking person renouncing the world to enter a religious order appealed to the romantic side of Cézanne's nature which was dominant at this time, when he painted many story-telling pictures, with titles such as *The Rape, The Murder, The Orgy.* This contrast is brought out in the color scheme: areas of rich, dark flesh color hemmed in on all sides by cold greys and whites. The brush stroke also contributes. It is rough and free, much of the paint being applied with the palette knife. Cézanne, under the influence of Courbet, deliberately used it to get away from the oily, over-finished surface of the fashionable Salon paintings which he despised. The broad and simple composition foreshadows his later work. Here the forms of head and hands already begin to be reduced to basic oval shapes repeated, as in the hood and the face, and emphasized by strong black outlines.

PLATE 10

Painted about 1870

THE BLACK CLOCK

Collection Mr. and Mrs. Edward G. Robinson,
Beverly Hills, California

21¼ x 28¾"

This is an early example of Cézanne's efforts to express human emotion by means of the simplest subject matter. Painted while he was still young and preoccupied with romantic ideas, this canvas depends for its effect on a series of contrasts. In the still life the fantastic shape of the shell with its gaping red mouth contrasts with everyday objects, such as the clock, vase, and coffee cup. The violent oppositions of light and dark give the picture a dramatic look—possibly Cézanne deliberately omitted the hands of the clock to add a feeling of suspense. The color scheme of a broad, whitish expanse surmounted by sharp accents of red and yellow, all set against a blue-black background, emphasizes this mood. The brushwork is broad and rather rough, showing the influence of Manet, who was greatly admired by Cézanne and his friends at this time.

The combination of these elements gives the picture a feeling of intense conviction, a quality which Cézanne's work retained throughout his life.

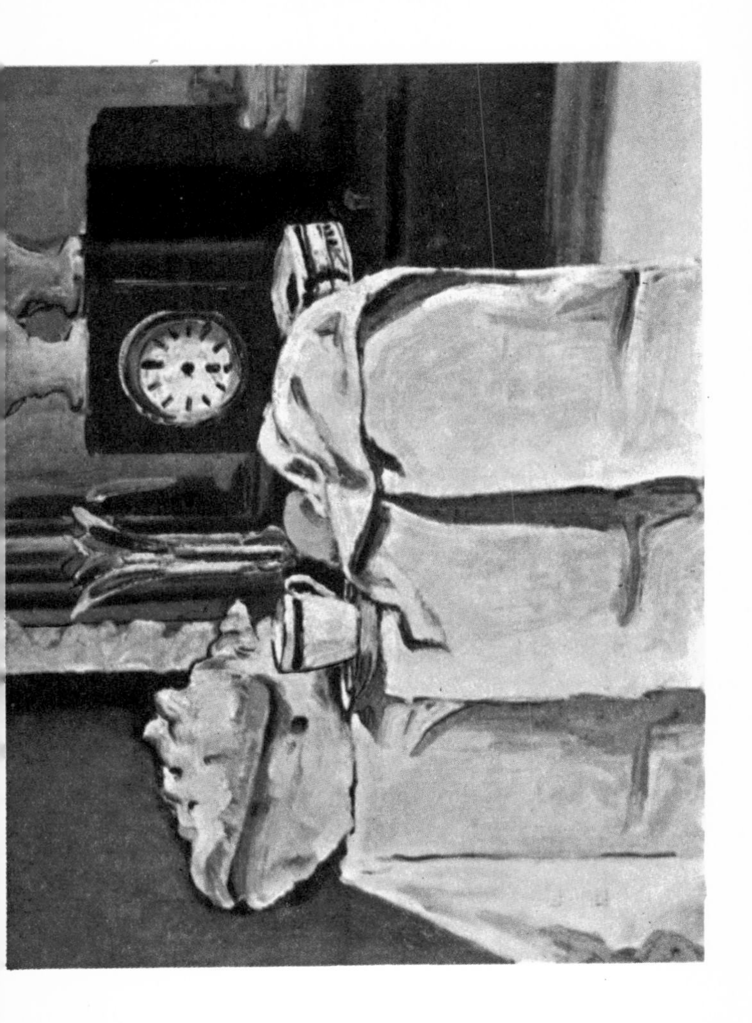

PLATE II

Painted about 1877

CHOCQUET SEATED

Columbus Gallery of Fine Arts, Ohio

18⅛ x 15"

Victor Chocquet was a minor customs official who loved painting, had a collection of Delacroix, and bought the work of Cézanne and Renoir while they were still ignored or despised by the critics and the public. Both artists painted him; Cézanne did five times. This little painting was probably intended as a sketch, and no effort is made to treat the sitter in detail; nevertheless, it is successful in portraying a reserved, sensitive, and independent personality.

In its bright coloring and in the broad dabs of paint of approximately equal size, this picture shows the influence of Pissarro, with whom Cézanne was working at this time. However, it already shows certain elements of Cézanne's mature style. These are the clarity of definition of the objects in the picture, and the reduction of these to simple, basic shapes—chiefly rectangular—which are repeated. Another of these elements is the emphasis on the surface: the two-dimensional composition of the painting. Although the figure is convincingly modeled in the round, the treatment of the colors and the way in which different forms are brought together bind it to the background so that the integrity of the surface is never broken.

Plate 12. MONT SAINTE-VICTOIRE (*commentary follows color plate se*

PLATE 13

Painted about 1885

VILLAGE OF GARDANNE

Brooklyn Museum, New York

36¼ x 28¾"

Cézanne loved to paint this little village perched on a hilltop a few miles south of Aix, where he had spent some time with his wife and baby at the time when his family still refused to agree to his marriage. The roof tops of the houses, leading up gradually to the church which stands above them, gave him a wonderful opportunity to paint the sort of clear and solid composition which he preferred. Each house and tree is like an architectural element built into a larger structure.

The unfinished state of the picture gives an interesting insight into Cézanne's working method. It shows how carefully his picture was planned, so that in spite of being incomplete, its basic structure and balance are already established. In the areas which have been barely touched by the brush, we see how he began with a slight transparent wash, subtly varied in tone, and then gradually added to this, using a new shade for almost every stroke. The areas of uncovered canvas with their light, almost stenographic touches of the brush give the picture a gaiety and carefree quality which is rare in his more finished works.

PLATE 14

Painted 1883–1887

MADAME CEZANNE

Collection Henry P. McIlhenny, Philadelphia, Pa.

24⅜ x 20⅛"

Little is known about Cézanne's married life. He met his wife during the early days in Paris, and soon afterward their son was born. Cézanne stuck to her in spite of his father's disapproval, and after a few years he finally obtained his parent's consent to the marriage. However, they gradually drifted apart, and toward the end of his life they were completely separated.

One need do no more than look at the sad and plaintive face in this portrait to know that she was not happy. We wonder how much her long-suffering expression may be due to having been forced to pose too long. Cézanne was terribly tyrannical in this respect and insisted on complete immobility; he said: "Sit like an apple. Does an apple move?"

The painting combines sensitivity to human feeling with formalized abstract design, particularly in the pure linear oval outline of the face. The soft curving lines of the dress, which are repeated in the hair, give a certain tender grace to the picture. This is also the result of the over-all harmony of pale blues and pinks.

PLATE 15

Painted 1890–1892

THE CARD PLAYERS

The Louvre, Paris

17¾ x 22½"

The subject of this painting of two peasants playing cards was probably inspired by a similar composition by one of the brothers Le Nain, French painters of the seventeenth century whose work Cézanne admired. He painted several versions of the subject, and there are numerous study drawings for both of the figures in this picture. His models were peasants from the neighboring farms, and he has painted them with a deep understanding of the simplicity and strength of their characters. There are no picturesque story-telling details; yet their thoughtful faces and bent shoulders tell us all about them, almost as if we were reading a chapter in Balzac.

The character of the peasants is emphasized by the use of arbitrary shadows to strengthen outlines, as in the head and hat of the man on the right. The rich color harmony of reddish browns and blues is wonderfully suited to the representation of these men whose lives are devoted to working the land. The composition, made up of a series of interlocking triangles and rectangles, has a weight and solidity which also makes an important contribution to the general character of the picture.

LIFT FOLD FOR ENTIRE PAINTING →

DETAIL AT RIGHT

PLATE 16

Painted about 1885–1887

THE BATHER

Museum of Modern Art, New York

50 x 38⅛"

All through his life Cézanne studied the nude figure and wanted to master it. When he was not copying paintings in the Louvre, he was sketching statues like *The Slaves* of Michelangelo or the *Milo* of Puget. Sometimes he sketched his own friends or soldiers bathing. However, owing probably to his extreme shyness, he refused to hire models. This made it impossible for him to analyze the human body as thoroughly as he did the forms of inanimate objects, which he could keep before him indefinitely.

This *Bather* is full of contrasting elements. It is realistic in the painting of the bathing trunks, the awkward anatomy, and differences in skin color. Some of the forms, such as the head, the shoulders and arms, are simplified almost to the abstract, and Cézanne has concentrated on reducing certain shapes to near geometric forms, the spaces between the arms and the body, for instance. The resulting effect, in spite of a certain hesitating and awkward quality, is serious and strong and leads us to believe that if he had attained the ideal for which he was striving, it might have had some resemblance to a Greek statue of the archaic period.

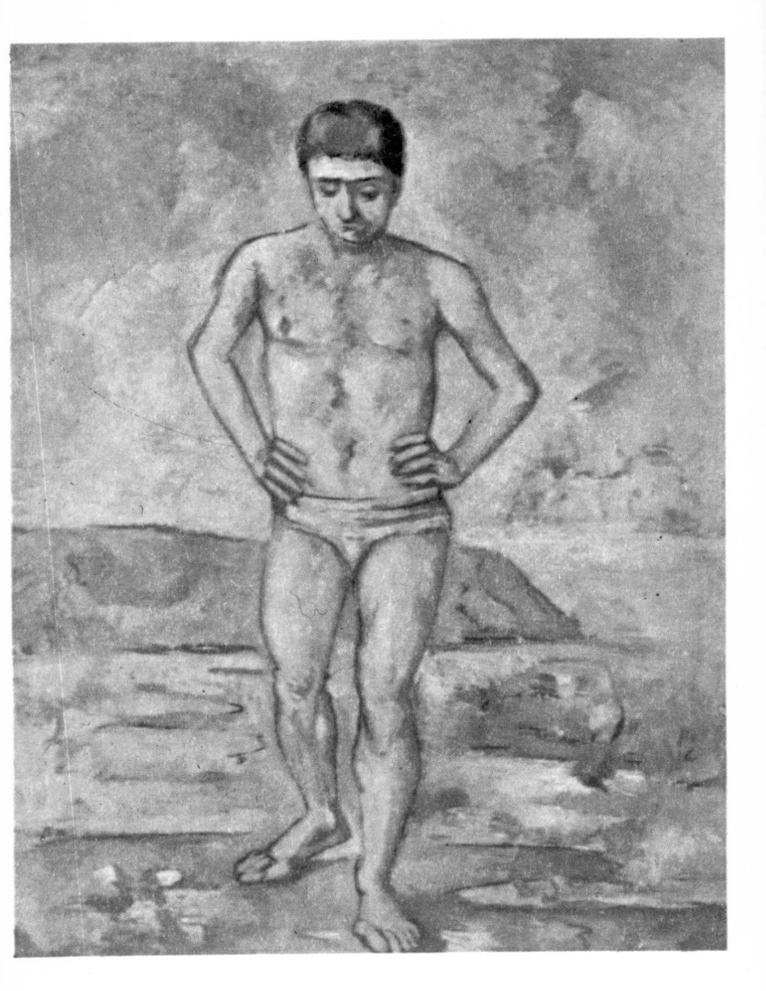

PLATE 17

Painted 1883–1887

THE BLUE VASE

The Louvre, Paris

24 x 19⅝"

Cézanne rarely succeeded in producing the feeling of brightness and gaiety which radiates from this beautiful picture. The subject—a vase, a bottle, some flowers and fruit—he painted many times; but here, as always, the new arrangement has a distinct personality of its own.

The mood of the picture is due to its color scheme. The prevailing tone of blue against which they are set gives extraordinary intensity to the red, green, and yellow tones and, by contrast, makes it possible for the light foreground and strip to the right to bring the feeling of sunshine into the picture. The infinite variety of texture, tone, and intensity which Cézanne has given to the one color blue shows how great a colorist he was. Though setting a blue vase and blue irises against a blue background, he has made the different objects stand out as sharply as if they were set against a complementary color. The comparative lack of finish and the broken outlines of the apples to the right and of the bottle contribute indirectly to concentrating attention on the vase and the flowers, the outlines of which are sharp and finished.

Plate 18. STILL LIFE WITH BASKET OF APPLES (*commentary follo*

plate section)

PLATE 19

Painted in 1888

ROAD AT CHANTILLY

Collection William A. M. Burden, New York

31⅞ x 25⅝"

Views of buildings, seen in the distance through an alley of trees, have been treated by landscape painters of all periods. Cézanne's interpretation of this subject is full of poetry. We feel the sunlight on the pink courtyard before the houses, the rich, waving foliage, and the cool shadows in the alley. And yet, we find that the canvas has an architectural structure in surface and in depth quite different from the work of other painters. The trees form a solid mass on either side of the alley; and although we have an impression of distance, the perspective lines of the alley have been treated so as to bring the buildings forward and to prevent completely any feeling of real distance, of a hole in the middle of the canvas. We are made conscious of the entire scene at one time. We are not invited in to wander about, as we would be in a landscape by Hobbema, for instance. The same effect is created by the color. The greens and blues in the trees are close in intensity to the colors of the houses, which minimizes the effect of distance and produces an over-all pattern, somewhat like a tapestry, on the surface of the canvas.

PLATE 20

Painted 1895–1900

STILL LIFE WITH ONIONS AND BOTTLE

The Louvre, Paris

26 x 31⅞"

This still life is characteristic of Cézanne's mature work. Of all his paintings it is one of the most serene in spirit and the most perfectly balanced in execution. There are no strains, no sharp contrasts; all the problems have been successfully solved. It is a complete statement.

The color harmony is restrained and subtle. There are no brilliant colors. The soft pinks and greens of the onions blend easily with the atmospheric blue of the background. The drawing is unusually effortless. All the outlines are continuous and flowing, from the curves of the table front to the graceful onion stems which lead the eye upward into the blue. And yet there is no lack of strength. The table is a solid base for the composition. There is real body to the drapery, and each onion is defined with clarity and modeled convincingly in the round. The bottle has the stability of a column.

The noblest human sentiment has been expressed by means of the humblest subject matter. A painting such as this might well inspire what one critic said of Cézanne during his lifetime: "He is a Greek of the great period."

LIFT FOLD FOR ENTIRE PAINTING →

DETAIL AT RIGHT

PLATE 22

Painted 1890–1894

TULIPS AND APPLES

The Art Institute of Chicago

23 x 16½"

This still life could almost be called a vocabulary of Cézanne's language in his mature period. The subject is expressed in terms of the utmost simplicity and, at the same time, the maximum conviction. The vase of flowers has been placed so that we see it as in a close-up. This is done by turning up the table surface arbitrarily, and by making the leaves of the tulips pass beyond the outer edge of the canvas. Each object—the apples, the vase, the table—is reduced to the simplest shape. With the exception of the smaller flowers, there is a complete lack of detail, and yet we are intensely aware of the identity of each one of the objects represented. The space in which they stand is clearly expressed, and we feel the air behind the flowers and the table. However, the tilting of the table surface already referred to, and the intensity of the color of the apple which is half hidden by the vase, create a bond between the surface and the background of the picture which strengthens the two-dimensional composition. The over-all brightness and liveliness are due to the color composition of contrasting reds and greens, and to the intensity of these colors.

AT RIGHT: DETAIL OF COVER PLATE

PLATE 23

Painted 1892–1894

THE HOUSE WITH CRACKED WALLS

Collection Mr. and Mrs. Ira Haupt, New York

25⅝ x 21¼"

Toward the end of his life Cézanne returned to the romanticism of his early youth. This landscape was painted at the beginning of that period and is unusual in his work because its dramatic effect is produced by an anecdotal detail, the dark crack running vertically through the wall, rather than by the general treatment of colors and forms. The result is more theatrical than usual.

The crack seems to have its root in a larger break at the base of the big rock to the right. The contrast between the size and permanence of this rock and the weaker structure of the little house, together with the thin tree trunks and the rather low and pale horizon line, combine to give the impression of a barren wilderness, which is further emphasized by the crisscross pattern of the vegetation and rocks in the foreground and the windswept branches of the trees to the left. The dark green silhouette of the pine tree behind the house adds to the dramatic effect produced by the black window and the gaping crack.

PLATE 24

Painted 1898–1900

WOODS WITH MILLSTONE

Collection Mr. and Mrs. Carroll S. Tyson, Philadelphia

29 x 36¼"

Cézanne painted this scene representing an abandoned quarry in the woods not far from his own house near Aix. Towards the end of his life, this was the sort of place which best suited his bitter and melancholy mood. Like Poussin, by placing the blocks of stone which have geometrical shapes in the foreground, he has given this part of the picture a certain intellectual clarity and balance. However, the waving lines of the tree trunks and the free treatment of the heavy foliage give the impression of a wilderness. It is this contrast between the calm and rational and the wild and instinctive which gives the picture its character.

The restrained color harmony of browns, greens, and dulled blues, without any touches of vivid color, maintains the over-all unity of the composition and is admirably suited to the atmosphere of the scene.

LIFT FOLD FOR ENTIRE PAINTING →
DETAIL AT RIGHT

PLATE 27

Painted 1895

STILL LIFE WITH CUPID

Courtauld Institute of Art, London

28 x 22½"

One of Cézanne's most graceful and charming works, it is, when analyzed, also one of the most interesting and surprising. In conjunction with a still life of apples, onions, and drapery, it contains two of his favorite models, plaster casts of a small Cupid by Puget and a statue of a flayed man (an anatomical study figure) once attributed to Michelangelo.

The Cupid is strongly modeled in the round and stands firmly on a table with brightly colored apples and onions at his feet. Behind him there is a view of the studio with paintings leaning against the walls. But Cézanne has arbitrarily transformed the lines of scientific perspective. By breaking the outline of the canvas behind the statue and emphasizing the roundness of the pear or apple lying in the corner, he has counteracted the effect of depth and maintained the integrity of the surface of the painting. This deliberate and closely-knit union of all the parts of a picture, was one of the qualities he admired so much in Poussin and tried so hard to attain himself. The simplification of forms to almost geometric patterns of circles and angles has been one of the chief sources of inspiration for the Cubist painters of our times.

PLATE 28

Painted about 1900

SELF-PORTRAIT WITH BERET

Museum of Fine Arts, Boston

25⅝ x 21¼"

Painted when he was in his sixties, this self-portrait is one of Cézanne's strongest and most successful. It is dispassionate and yet highly sensitive. It shows him sad and bitter as he had gradually become, and even gives a feeling of his loneliness. The eyes look at nothing, the face is sullen and yet extremely alive. The portrait tells the whole story of his disappointments, his isolation, and his great stubbornness, with extraordinary intensity.

It is painted in a wonderful harmony of blues and reds, ranging from touches that are exquisitely pale and delicate to passages of great depth and resonance. In this richness and variety within such a limited color range, Cézanne shows himself to be the equal of Rembrandt and Delacroix.

In contrast to the richness of the color, the structure and drawing are composed of a few forms of the utmost simplicity which are repeated throughout. The curve of the top of the beret occurs again in the forehead, in the ear, and again in the line of the shoulders. The sharp angular shape of the nose, which is so expressive, is repeated in the moustache, in the goatee, and again in the white collar.

COMMENTARY FOR

COLOR PLATE 12

Painted 1885–1887

MONT SAINTE-VICTOIRE

The Metropolitan Museum of Art, New York

25⅝ x 31⅞"

The Mont Sainte-Victoire dominates all the countryside around Aix like a huge marble pyramid. The people of the region foretell the weather by the way it looks and have certain superstitious beliefs about it. Cézanne painted it over and over again, and at the end of his life it had become almost his only model.

In this perfect example of his mature art, the mountain is partly hidden by trees and takes its place with the other forms in the landscape. The shrubbery and the trees in the foreground, and the wall of mountains and hills in the distance, create between them a crystal-clear body of space in the center, the quality of which is emphasized by the pale blue sky.

The color shows Cézanne's complete mastery of landscape painting, ranging, always with incredible variety, from the brightest greens to the pale blue-pink in the distance, and always composed in order to keep the unity of the picture. The drawing is of the utmost simplicity: tree trunks are almost cylinders, foliage is made up by brush strokes in abstract shapes which nevertheless are completely convincing in their suggestion of nature.

COMMENTARY FOR

COLOR PLATE 18

Painted 1890–1894

STILL LIFE WITH BASKET OF APPLES

The Art Institute of Chicago

24⅜ x 31"

Cézanne was very meticulous about composing his still life, and, like the Dutch masters of the seventeenth century whose work he studied in the Louvre, he carefully propped up the basket on a block or set the angle of an apple with a coin, until he had exactly what he wanted. The result is a cheerful and rather sunny painting. However, its effect is quite different from what we find in the still life painting of other great painters. When Chardin, for example, paints fruit, he gives the texture of each surface so that we feel that we could eat it. Each one of Cézanne's apples is very definitely, almost aggressively, an apple, but its appeal is to our minds rather than to our appetites. It is a description of an apple in the simplest, most essential terms.

The composition is made to carry our attention to the apples in the folds of the napkin lying on the table. Everything leads to this—the tipped-up basket, the angle of the lady-fingers, the folds of the napkin, the bottle like a dark exclamation point in the center. However, the richness and vitality of the picture are due to the brilliant color, the unexpected contrasts, and the sharp accents and vibrating, broken lines of the drawing.

Plate 29. THE MOWER. *1875-76. Pencil*
Collection Mr. and Mrs. Ira Haupt, New York

Plate 30. BOY IN A RED WAISTCOAT. *1890-95. Water color*
Collection Mr. and Mrs. W. Feilchenfeldt, Zurich

Plate 31. THE BATHERS. *1890-1900. Lithograph*
Museum of Modern Art, New York

Plate 32. STUDY FOR THE CARD PLAYERS. *1890-92. Water color*
Collection Chauncey McCormick, Chicago

Plate 33. TWO STUDIES OF THE ARTIST'S SON. *1877-78. Pencil*
The Art Institute of Chicago (Arthur Heun Fund)

Plate 34. STUDY AFTER PUGET'S "CUPID." *1895-1900. Water color*
Collection Sam Salz, New York

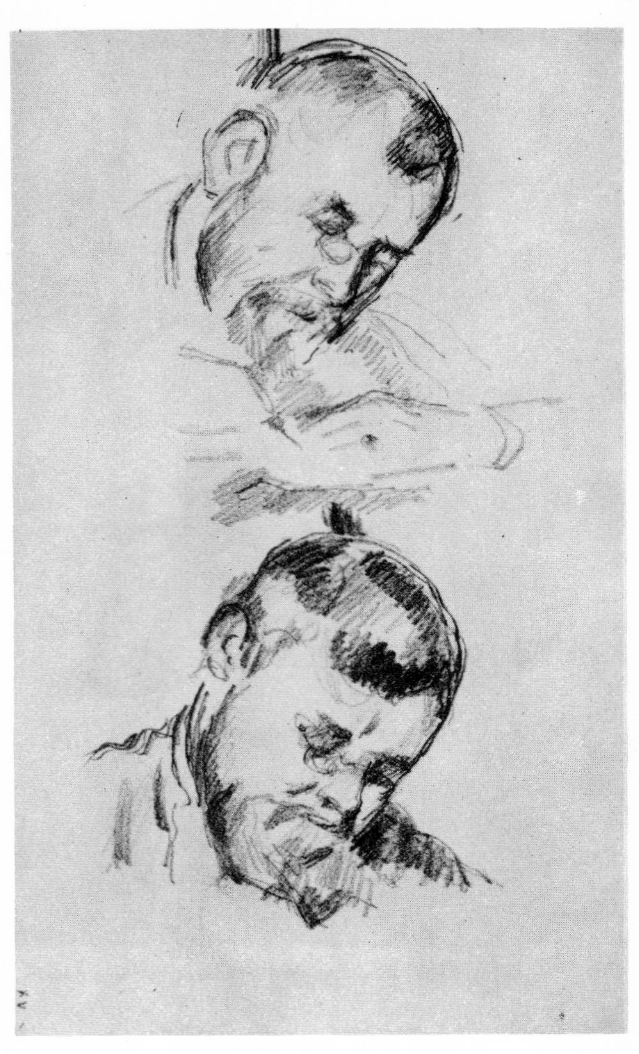

Plate 36. TWO STUDIES OF EMILE ZOLA. *1879-85. Pencil*
Collection Mr. and Mrs. Leigh B. Block, Chicago

Plate 37. BATHERS. *1883-87. Pencil. Collection Mr. and Mrs. Ira Haupt, New York*

Plate 38. STUDY OF SKULLS. *1885. Water color*
Collection Erich Maria Remarque, New York

Plate 39. HARLEQUIN. *1888. Pencil and wash*
Collection Mr. and Mrs. Ira Haupt, New York

BIOGRAPHICAL NOTES

1839	Paul Cézanne (pronounced *say-ZANN*) born January 10, Aix-en-Provence, France.
1852–58	Becomes close friend of Emile Zola at school in Aix. Father sends him to law school.
1861–64	Studies art in Paris; associates with Renoir, Pissarro, Sisley, Monet.
1870	Goes south to L'Estaque to avoid service in Franco-Prussian War; lives with Hortense Fiquet, who bears him a son two years later.
1874–78	Exhibits with the Impressionists, but gradually loses sympathy with their aims. His work ridiculed by critics and public.
1884	His family allows marriage to Hortense.
1886	Breaks with Zola whose portrayal of him as the heroic failure of his novel *L'Oeuvre* wounded Cézanne deeply.
1900	Exhibits at Paris World's Fair. His following and reputation begin to grow.
1904	Exhibition of thirty-three paintings at Salon d'Automne is a major vindication of his art.
1906	Catches severe chill while painting and dies in Aix-en-Provence, October 22.
1907	Important retrospective exhibition of fifty-six paintings at Salon d'Automne.

CEZANNE ON ART

"I am the primitive of a new art."

"The realization of my sensation is always very difficult. I cannot attain the intensity that is unfolded before my senses."

"Drawing and color are not distinct. . . . When color is richest, form is finest."

"Represent nature by means of the cylinder, the sphere, the cone, all placed in perspective."

"Every time I come away from Poussin, I know myself better. . . . I wish to make Poussin live again, according to nature."

"Chardin understood that objects are in contact with each other through intimate reflected colors, just as we are through our speech and our eyesight."

"In the museum, the painter learns to think; before nature, he learns to see. It is absurd to imagine that we grow like mushrooms when we have all those generations behind us. Why not take advantage of all their work."

"Our canvases are the milestones of Man—from the reindeer on the walls of caves to the cliffs of Monet—from the hunters, the fishermen who inhabit the tombs of Egypt, the comical scenes of Pompeii, the frescoes of Pisa and Siena, the mythological compositions of Veronese and Rubens, from all these the same spirit comes down to us. . . . We are all the same man. I shall add another link to this chain of color. My own blue link."

SOME OTHER BOOKS ABOUT CEZANNE

Cézanne, (Introduction by M. Reynard). London, Fama, 1948
(Collection of Paintings)

Paintings, (Introduced by Benedict Nicolson). London, Drummond, 1946

Paul Cézanne, (Text by Meyer Schapiro). London, Thames and Hudson, 1952

ROGER FRY. *Cézanne : A Study of his Development.* London, Hogarth Press, 1927

EDWARD ALDEN JEWELL. *Paul Cézanne.* London, Simpkin, 1947

GERSTLE MACK. *Paul Cézanne.* New York, Alfred A. Knopf, 1935
(Popular, standard biography)

LIONELLO VENTURI. *Cézanne.* Paris, Paul Rosenberg, 1936
(Complete catalogue of paintings and graphic work)

PRINTED IN HOLLAND
OFFSET SMEETS WEERT